THE ART

OF

PEN - AND - INK DRAWING,

COMMONLY CALLED

ETCHING.

BY

H. R. ROBERTSON,

Fellow of the Society of Painter Etchers; Author of "The Art of Etching," "Life on the Upper Thames," &c.

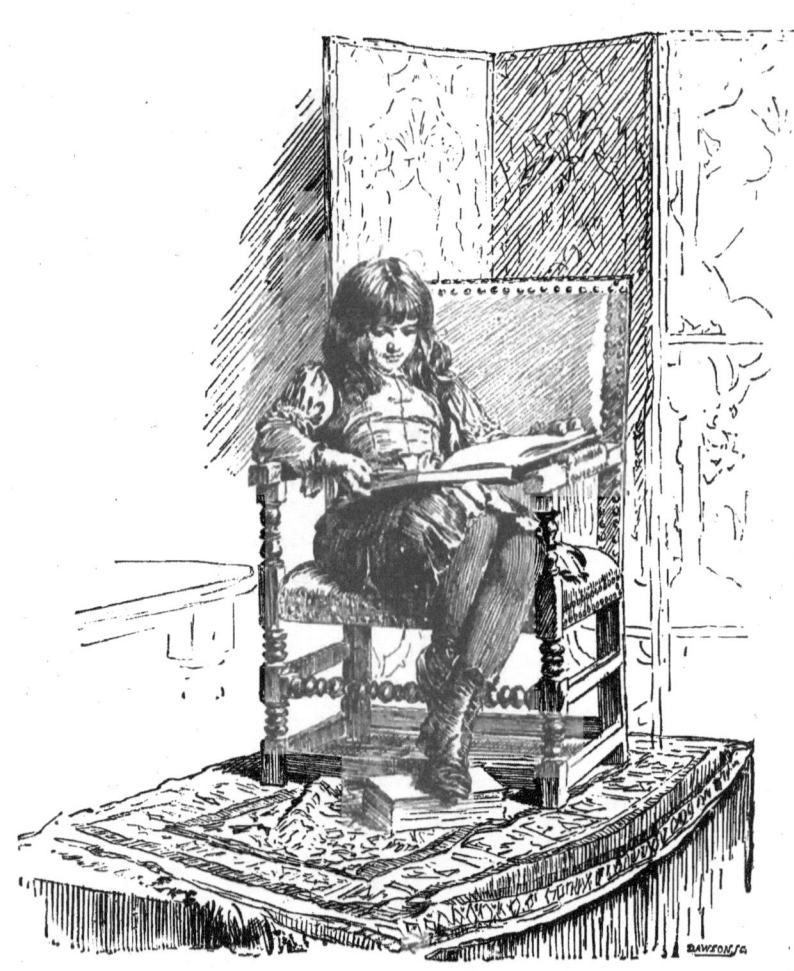

THE SANCTUM INVADED.—*E. J. Gregory, A.R.A.*

CONTENTS.

ILLUSTRATIONS.

PREFACE.

WHILE dividing this little treatise into the three parts, the theory of Pen-and-Ink Drawing, its practice, and its application to the reproductive processes, I have found that the degree in which these separate divisions overlap each other, has prevented the arrangement being quite so satisfactory as I could have wished.

I have much pleasure in expressing my sincere thanks to Sir Frederick Leighton, P.R.A., Sir John Gilbert, R.A., Vicat Cole, R.A., Professor Herkomer, A.R.A., G. H. Boughton, A.R.A., E. J. Gregory, A.R.A., and the other artists who have kindly consented to my using illustrations made by them for various purposes, and to the editors and publishers of 'Academy Notes,' 'The Art Journal,' and the 'Magazine of Art.'

The illustrations have been selected principally with the view of showing how much may be expressed with few lines, such examples being, in my opinion, the most conducive to the formation of a

good style. I regret that in one or two instances
we have been obliged to be content with part of
the original woodcut instead of the whole. The
small size of our page has necessitated the cutting
down in these cases ; but as our purpose is rather
to show manner of execution than anything else,
the loss is not of such moment as it might otherwise have been.

PEN-AND-INK DRAWING.

GENERAL REMARKS.

THE suitability of the pen as an instrument for the use of a beginner is thus ably advocated by Mr. Ruskin :—" It is better to take in early practice some instrument with a hard and fine point, both that we may give some support to the hand, and that by working over the subject with so delicate a point, the attention may be properly directed to all the most minute parts of it. Even the best artists need occasionally to study subjects with a pointed instrument, in order thus to discipline their attention ; and a beginner must do so for a considerable period." The superiority of work done with pen and ink over that produced with the black lead pencil, consists in its much more extended range of tone, and its total freedom from unpleasant shine in the darks.

When the question arises as to what examples a beginner should copy who wishes to practise the art of pen and ink drawing, the difficulty will be to select from the great and varied stores of material that everywhere abound to his hand. All steel and copper-plate engravings that have been executed in line and all wood engravings are within the *possible* range of pen and ink drawing. Those woodcuts in which the white lines play a prominent part must of course be excepted as being obviously unsuited for the purpose. I hold, however, that much time should not be devoted to the imitative copying of prints, only indeed so much as enables the student to learn with what arrangement of lines the different textures and qualities of objects in nature may be best rendered. The common attempt to make a pen-and-ink drawing absolutely imitative of a line engraving has its precise equivalent in those remarkable feats of penmanship that are executed with the hope of extorting from the beholder the transcendent compliment that they "might pass for copperplate!" I have lately noticed that certain of the popular magazines have offered prizes for the best imitative copies in pen-and-ink of engravings after well-known pictures. One would not wish to interfere with such an agreeable pastime ; but I cannot help protesting against the assurance often so confidently given by the editor of the journal to some successful competitor, that if he adopt the profession of the fine arts a brilliant career is before him. The fact of the matter is, that such proficiency, far from suggesting promise of distinction in the profession, plainly marks a tendency to mechanical pursuits, and is not at all likely to be acquired by any one with much instinctive feeling for the arts of design.

There are two distinct methods of obtaining effect with the pen—one by few lines laid slowly, and the other by many lines drawn with rapidity. If the intention is to see what effect may be obtained with comparatively few lines slowly and deliberately laid, we may refer from amongst the Old Masters to the woodcuts after Albert Durer and

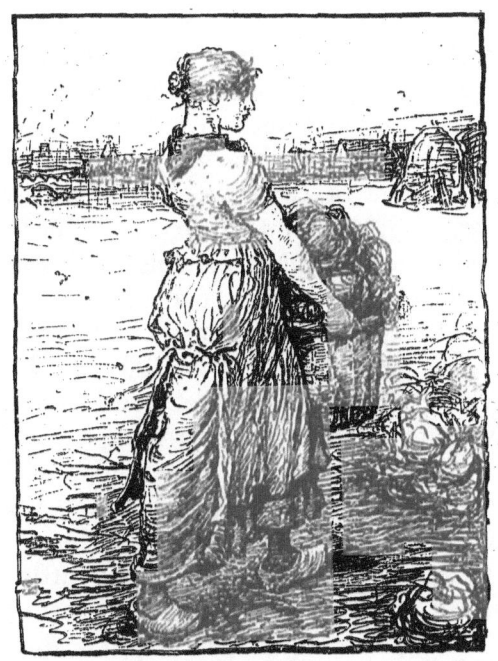

A Field Handmaiden, Brabant.—*G. H. Boughton, A.R.A.*

Holbein, and the line engraving of Marc Antonio. The engraved plates by Durer furnish us excellent examples of work with more and finer lines than his woodcuts. Some of the etchings of Rembrandt are on the other hand perfect samples of what may be fairly reproduced in pen-and-ink. In them we find the effect to depend upon innumerable lines in all directions. In the matter of landscape, the etched plates by Claude, Ruysdael and Waterloo are good examples for study, and in that of animal life we may refer to those of Paul Potter and Dujardin.

Of modern work which may be studied with advantage, Alfred Rethel's well-known designs, "Death the Friend," and "Death the Avenger," and the wood-cuts after F. Sandys are the best instances I know of extremely deliberate work in line corresponding in its way to the older work of Durer; while some of Millais' illustrations may be cited as instances of free execution where the direction of the line is apparently as little considered as by Rembrandt. The difference between such styles as those of Holbein and Rembrandt contains in its essence the contrasting ideal that in architecture distinguishes Renaissance from Gothic, and in literature the Romantic from the Classic.

For economy of line with extraordinary power of suggesting a great deal with very little work, perhaps Mr. Caldecott's designs rank as high as any: his delightful books for children always repay one for a reiterated perusal. The illustrations by Adolf Menzel to the life of Frederick the Great are perfect mines of study, and have had an obvious influence, directly or indirectly, on all artists since his work appeared. It is the drawings in the latter half of the book that are so particularly fine, the artist's ability seeming to grow as he proceeded

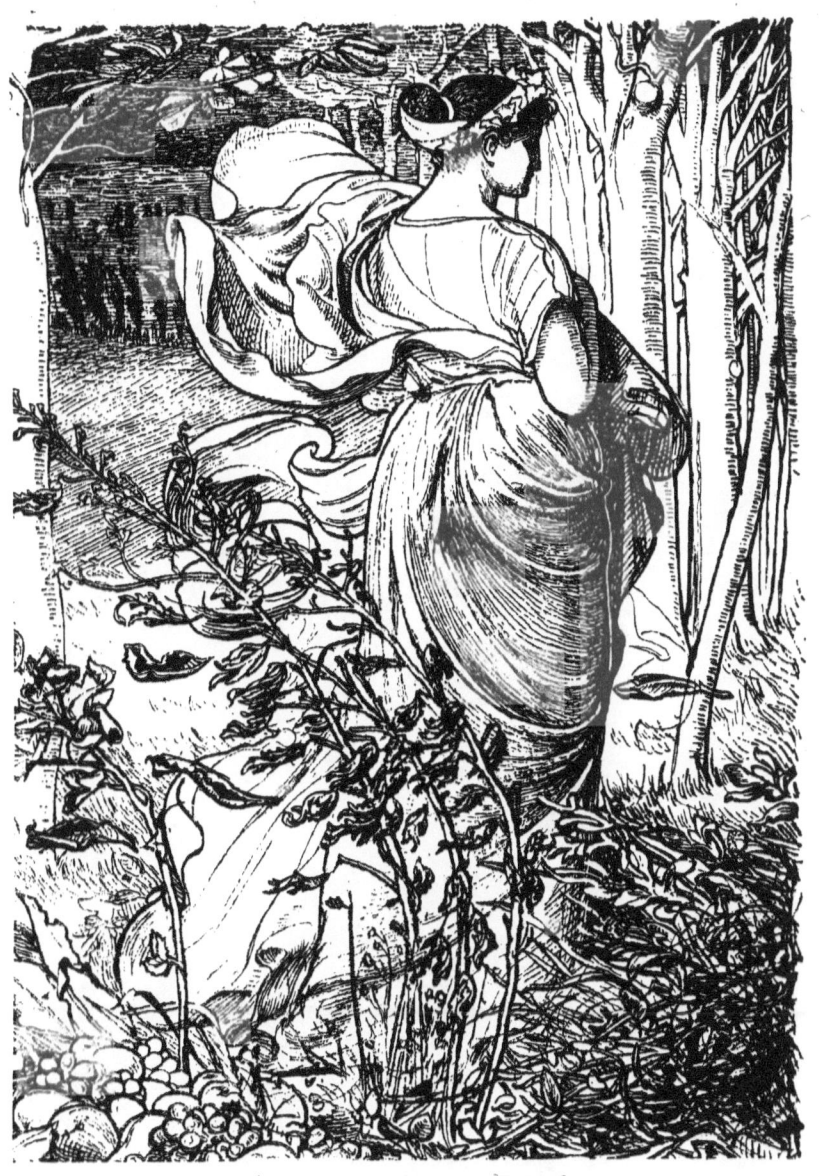

THE ADVENT OF WINTER.—*F. Sandys.*

with the undertaking, while the engravers gradually dropped their poor methods of translation for the simple endeavour to reproduce his masterly work in fac-simile. The large drawings by the same artist of Frederick the Great's generals are splendid examples for pen-and-ink practice. Our illustration by Lalauze after Frank Hals resembles much, in manner of execution, these fine heads by Menzel.

By the Old Masters the pen was usually employed for hastily sketching compositions of contemplated pictures, which were very rarely carried to any degree of imitative finish. The labour required for covering large spaces with a delicate tint was felt to be incommensurate with the result ; so that instead of obtaining it by this means, it was found better to add a wash with the brush. Bistre was the pigment most frequently used for the purpose. There are some beautiful designs for monumental sculpture by Rubens, executed in this manner ; examples are to be seen in the Peel collection of drawings exhibited in the basement rooms of the National Gallery. In the same rooms are placed the original drawings for Turner's Liber Studiorum, which are very fine specimens of the combination of wash and pen work. In most of these designs the pen is used for outlining objects, and for adding decision where it would assist the engraver who was to reproduce them in mezzotint. In some, as in the " Bonneville, Savoy," bold pen lines are used as shading in foliage, while zig-zag lines indicate reflections in the water. Prout also used

the reed-pen with brown ink to define forms, not
only in monochrome, but also in his water-colour
drawings.

; It is excellent practice to occasionally make pen-
and-ink studies very rapidly from nature without
any previous pencilling whatever. I have found

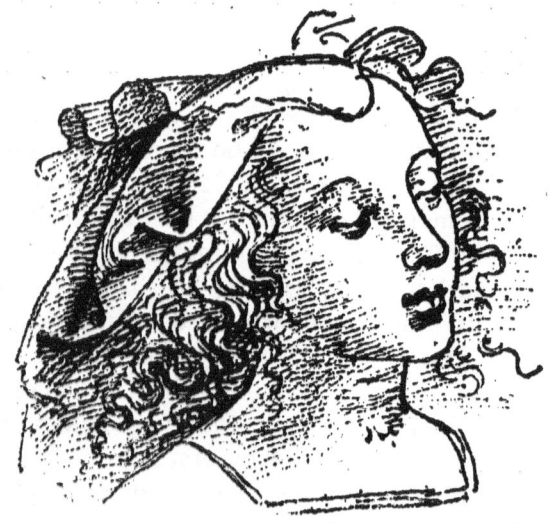

STUDY.—*Raphael.*

this equally useful in landscape or figure work ;
whether the motive is to make a memorandum of
effect, or to hit off a characteristic attitude, or one
intended to express movement. One of my fellow-
students used to join me in the exercise of making
such sketches with the definite time limit of ten
minutes. We often thus posed alternately for each

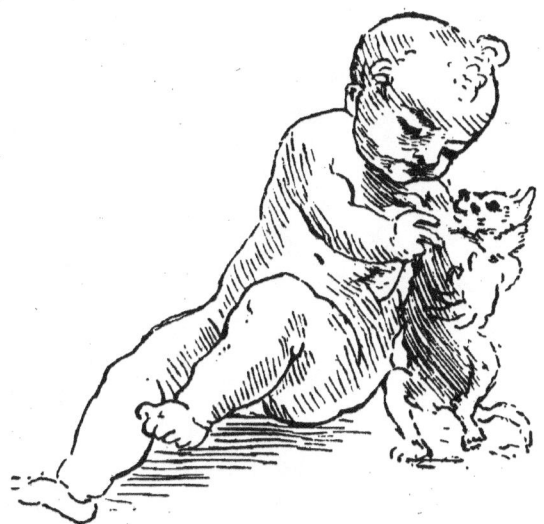

Study.—*Raphael.*

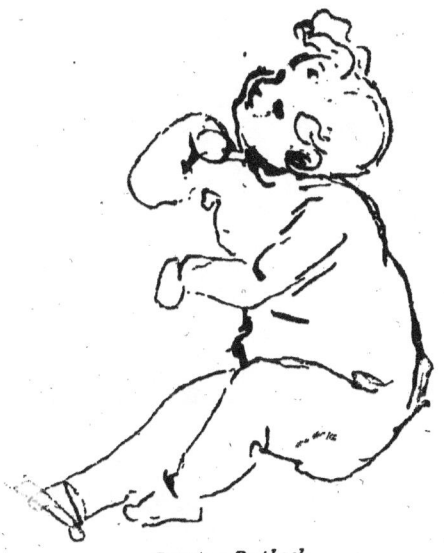

Study.—*Raphael.*

other, and we easily induced any chance visitor
who might look in to sit for us for the short time
named. By-the-bye, the seeming length of the ten
minutes is found to vary incredibly according to
whether one is drawing or posing. Studies made
thus are almost sure to err in matters of proportion, but are rarely deficient in emphasis. A great
philosophical writer has said that "Art is emphasis," and though, as a definition this is, of
course, incomplete ; yet it is a useful hint in these
days of photography, when so much work is rated
as finished in proportion to the degree in which all
emphasis is eliminated from it. Before com-
mencing a design, for a book illustration, for
instance, it is not a bad plan to make some pre-
liminary studies in this hurried manner ; and then
after the careful drawing has been completed with
all the finish that an unlimited bestowal of time
can effect, to compare the two. It will usually be
found that there is something in the first, unsatis-
factory as it seemed perhaps when just done, that
may with advantage be incorporated into the
second.

Mr. Ruskin has given students the following
valuable hints as to direction of line in shading.
" When the material or the time of the artist does
not permit him to make a perfect drawing—that is
to say, one in which no lines shall be prominently
visible—and he is reduced to show the black lines,
either drawn by the pen, or on the wood, it is
better to make these lines help, as far as may be,
the expression of texture and form. You will thus

find many textures, as of cloth or grass or flesh, and many subtle effects of light, expressed by Leech with zig-zag, or crossed, or curiously broken lines ; and you will see that Alfred Rethel and Richter constantly express the direction and rounding of surfaces by the direction of the lines which shade them. All these various means of expression will be useful to you, as far as you can learn them, provided you remember that they are merely a kind of short-hand, telling certain facts not in quite the right way, but in the only possible way under the conditions ; and provided in any after use of such means, you never try to show your own dexterity ; but only to get as much record of the object as you can in a given time ; and that you continually make efforts to go beyond such short-hand, and draw portions of the objects rightly.

And touching this question of direction of lines as indicating that of surface, observe these few points :

If lines are to be distinctly shown, it is better that, so far as they *can* indicate anything by their direction, they should explain rather than oppose the general character of the object. And Albert Durer, whose work was chiefly engraving, sets himself always thus to make his lines as *valuable* as possible, telling much by them, both of shade and direction of surface ; and if you were always to be limited to engraving on copper (and did not want to express effects of mist or darkness, as well as delicate forms), Albert Durer's way of work would be the best example for you. But inasmuch as the perfect way of drawing is by shade and without lines, and the great painters always conceive their subjects as complete, even when

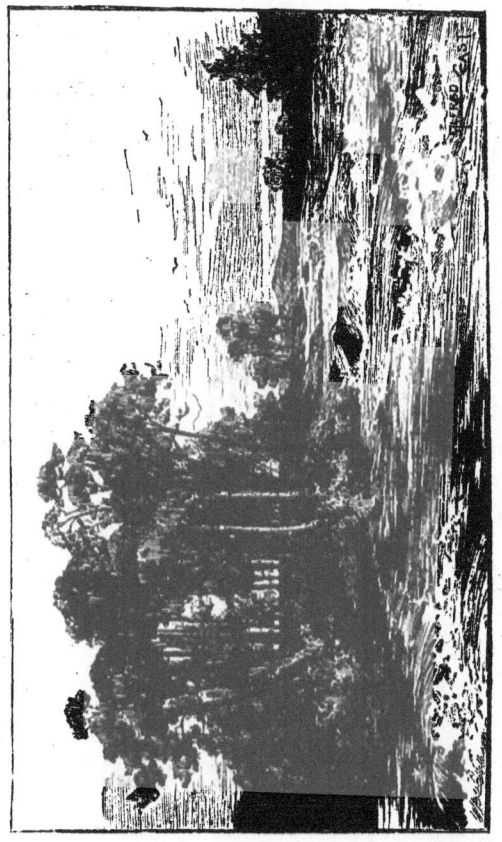

THE DARK ISLAND.—*Alfred East.*

they are sketching it most rapidly, you will find that, when they are not limited in means, they do not much trust to direction of line, but will often scratch in the shade of a rounded surface with nearly straight lines, that is to say, with the easiest and quickest lines possible to themselves. When the hand is free, the easiest line for it to draw is one inclining from the left upwards to the right, or *vice versâ* from the right downwards to the left; and when done very quickly, the line is hooked a little at the end by the effort at return to the next. Hence, you will always find the pencil, chalk, or pen-sketch of a *very* great master full of these kind of lines; and even if he draws carefully, you will find him using simple straight lines from left to right, when an inferior master would have used curved ones. Even the careful drawings of Leonardo da Vinci are shaded most commonly with straight lines; and you may always assume it as a point increasing the probability of a drawing being by a great master if you find rounded surfaces such as those of cheeks or lips, shaded with straight lines."

Our frontispiece, by Mr. E. J. Gregory, is an excellent example of simplicity in execution, the lines hardly ever being crossed, and yet a great deal of variety in tone and texture being attained. Such execution looks delightfully easy, but is not really so, as it presupposes that the artist knows exactly what the effect of every set of lines will be when the whole is completed.

While speaking of this simple execution, which consists mainly of one set of lines, approximately parallel, drawn in the manner most easy to the hand, we may refer from amongst modern work to the etched portraits by Legros, and to many of the drawings in *Punch* by Charles Keene. The direction of line adopted in these instances has been sometimes jocularly spoken of by artists amongst themselves as the north-west system of line-work. This method of execution comes naturally to the hand, as being but a slight modification of the down-stroke in writing.

Drawings shaded in this style often attain to a largeness of style hardly to be reached by more laborious methods of execution. This sense of style, unconsciously recalling the Old Masters, is a most valuable quality, and rare enough in our times to be highly appreciated by us. I do not, of course, claim that drawings executed in this manner necessarily suggest the Old Masters; the fact rather being that a simple and dignified manner of execution in any branch of the fine arts is generally the outcome of true feeling, such as animated the great masters.

The mental properties of every line drawn with the pen and ink or etching-needle, should be original and personal. As in the case of writing with the pen, we are often able to recognise at a glance the individual hand, so, and much more so, should it be with a drawing. Not that the draughtsman (any more than does the writer) should aim at making his hand-work recognisable by any affected peculiarity; but this strong point is sure to be attained unconsciously if an artist's work is simple and sincere, and not the mannered imitation of another's style.

We are happily emerging from the period when the idea of high art was associated with such hard characterless outlines as those of Retsch, and the many series in his manner issued by the Art Union of London—publications about as poor in intention as anything that was ever honoured by any such quasi-authoritative body. I cannot better explain my antipathy to all such examples of 'pure line' than by quoting Mr. Seymour Haden's explanation of what good drawing really is. "Good drawing, we may be told, is a correct expression of form by a line or a series of lines exactly laid down. I do not think it is. I think that good drawing is the correct representation of any object or series of objects, as they appear in nature; that is, the art of conveying on the flat a verisimilitude of what the eye sees in space; that it is an aggregation of values, a bringing into juxtaposition and harmony and relation and balance every one of the surfaces which compose a picture in relief. But planes and surfaces are not lines, and cannot be expressed by lines. The cube which is before us, the book which is upon the table, and the table itself, present us with certain facets which are in opposition, or in apposition, or at various angles one with another; but there is no line, or anything like a line, between any two of these facets. The cube asserts itself by the physical properties which belong to a cube; not by a line which divides it from the table, or the table from it, or it from surrounding objects. He, therefore, whose eye is sensible of the properties which belong to material

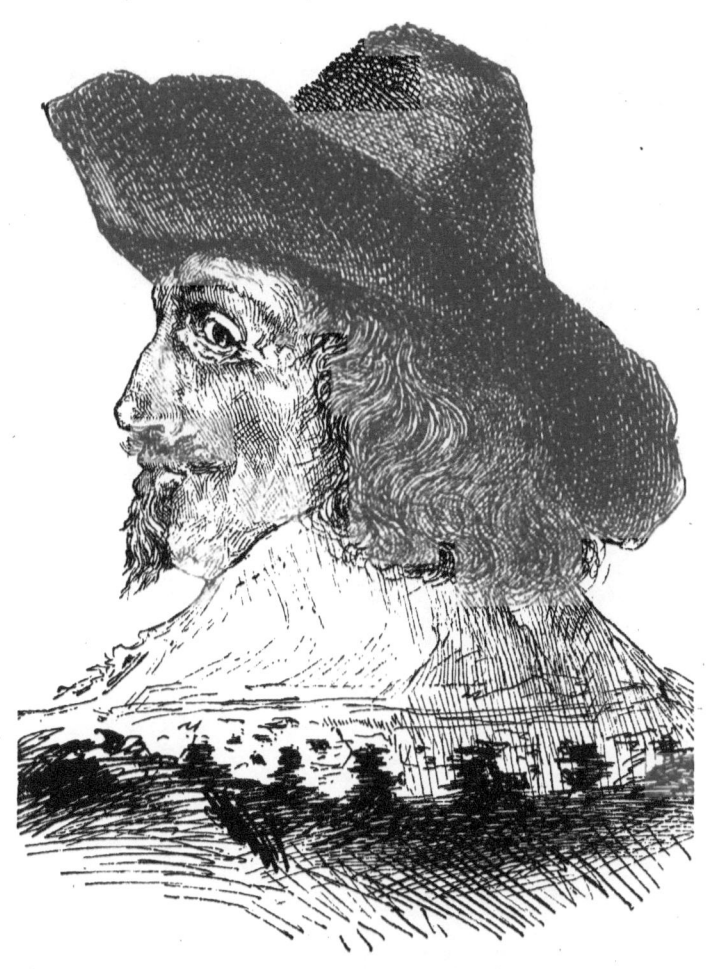

HEAD.—*La'auze, after Frank Hals.*

C

bodies, and of the relative value they bear to each other, and whose hand can express them—can draw them. He who fails to convey them in their reality, however legitimate and consecrated by usage his mode of procedure, cannot draw them. If, having made an exact outline of their forms, the *ensemble* of his work fails to convey this idea of their reality—he cannot draw them. The imaginary lines which compose the *contour* of the human hand, may be laid down with the utmost precision ; but if they fail, as they are likely to do, to convey the idea of the hand in its attribute as an active member of the body, they have not succeeded in drawing it ; whereas, a great master, or a great genius, who, by a process thrown off by his brain—he knows not how—holds it out to you, plants the thumb firmly on the table with a pressure which is to be felt, and gives it the exact relation which it should bear to the body of which it is a member, has drawn it."

One of the essential reasons why the Old Masters practised the art of etching on copper was the fact of its being the most available means then known for multiplying their designs, and of meeting the wishes of the extended circle of their admirers for examples of their art. Many of the truest lovers of art have in all ages been of those whose private means have not permitted them to purchase original pictures. Now, in our time, science has added a new method by which the designs of artists may be multiplied indefinitely and more cheaply than by copper-plate etching,—a pen-and-ink drawing, or a single impression of an etching, being all that is required from the hand of the artist. Photography, chemistry, and mechanical science in combination, furnish us with such admirable reproductions that it is now possible to possess fac-similes of the whole of the etched work of Rembrandt for a very moderate outlay; while the last volume of 'Academy Notes' gives the purchaser for a single shilling more than a hundred autographic sketches by his contemporaries. In the publication just named, and in that illustrating the *Salon*, it is very interesting to note the artistic individuality patent in such slight jottings of pictures, the slightness of these suggestive sketches being in many cases the very reason of their charm. There is the satisfaction to the artist, in making the original drawings for such a purpose, that he is "showing his hand," as Raphael called it when he wrote to Albert Dürer sending him some pen-and-ink drawings.

When making a pen-and-ink drawing, or any study in black and white (other than outline), there are two distinct motives which should be kept apart in the mind of the student, though in his work they are bound to overlap each other more or less. The first is the representation of the light and shade, and the second is the rendering of the local tones or colours. It is important to dwell on these two different aims, because I have often noticed an absolute confusion in the use of the terms amongst students and amateurs, such as is shown by the remark, " I thought the black and white of a picture meant the same thing as its light and shade." It might be objected by a purist, that, as different colours reflect light unequally, the translating of the colours into black and white is only rendering the light and shade ; but it is not generally so understood. A couple of examples will make my meaning more clear than any amount of explanation. In Mr. Charles Keene's

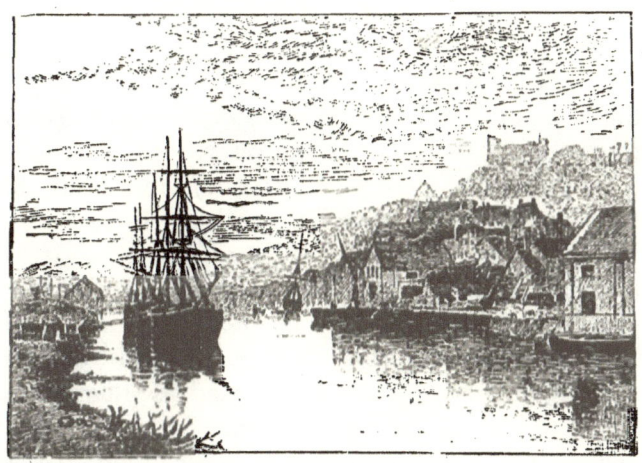

ARUNDEL.—*Vicat Cole, R.A.*

drawings in *Punch*, particularly in his early ones, he made no difference in the treatment of a black silk hat and a straw hat of pale yellow, or between a black coat and a smock frock ; every object having the half that turned towards the light left white, which is or nearly so, while the other half has a medium tint of lines to represent shade. If this treatment be contrasted with John Leech's, or more noticeably still, with Mr. Du Maurier's recent drawings, the difference that I mean will be seen at once. In the latter we find black coats represented as nearly uniformly dark, while a white shirt will be almost blank paper. I am not now contending that the one treatment is right and that the other is wrong, or even that in the abstract the one is superior to the other; at present I only wish the reader to clearly grasp the distinction indicated between the light and shade of a picture or drawing and its black and white. The purpose for which a drawing exists must always rule the conditions of its production ; and while on this subject, I would venture to remark that for the trivial purpose of illustrating a joke (often a very poor one), many of the drawings in *Punch* are of much too serious a style. While trying "to shoot Folly as she flies," let us not forget to draw the line at flying shots. Such precise draughtsmanship as shows unmistakeably that models must have been posed by the artist in the respective attitudes delineated, is inconsistent with the idea of satirical or comic drawing. At all events, this is the opinion of the best foreign artists, who, for similar reasons, do not always endorse our insular opinion with reference to many of Landseer's humorous subjects. While all allow that a joke in literature should seem spontaneous, and not laboured, it does not seem to be taken for granted that the same is the case in art,—that caricatures and humorous subjects should be lightly and easily sketched, never worked out laboriously, and therefore never painted in oils, with weeks of labour. A picture or engraving on the walls of a sitting-room that has been purchased for its humorous quality, must, one would think, become as great a bore as an inmate of the house who should repeat the same old joke daily. Publishers, however, all agree in their experience that an engraved plate of a humorous subject is the best of properties; seeming indeed to fulfil the average Philistine's idea of 'a joy for ever.' If the student should have a turn for drawing caricatures with pen and ink, let him remember that they should look when done as if it had been only fun to him to do them; the joke once expressed, all other facts are superfluous, and indeed detrimental. Leech, Caldecott, and Busch are perhaps the best masters to be studied in this branch of modern art.

As in painting the quality most essential is colour, so in pen-and-ink drawing or etching, it is the suggestion of colour which is the most important. The main reasons for this seem to be, firstly, that we see all objects in nature as variously coloured masses, our perception of the local colour remaining through all the changes of light and shade; secondly, that the light and shade is more subject throughout to fixed rules than the colour, and so the translating of the different colours of a picture into black and white shows us infinite varieties of subtle and broken tones with occasionally startling and pleasing surprises. The superior value in art of colour over light and shade was insisted on by Leonardo da Vinci, who recommended to his pupils that they should paint the effect on the model as seen "under an awning in a courtyard, on dull days, or by twilight."

There are however some cases in which the light and shade and the black and white of a subject are pretty nearly identical in tone ; as, for instance, in the portrayal of sculpture, or in the representation of an interior lighted from a single small window, and where the principal objects happen to be draperies and furniture of a lightish colour. In the latter case we are always grateful for such a point of dark value as is given by a head of black hair, or of light value as a white cap ; because they tend to give suggestions of delicate colour to the rest of the picture.

Though, according to the much-quoted definition, finish in painting may mean " added fact," yet it is by no means the case in pen-and-ink drawing or etching. It is indeed an apparent negligence of most facts resulting in the total omission of very many, and subtle emphasis on those most worthy of consideration that constitute the basis of its claim to be fine art at all. Many of the etchings of Rembrandt, Seymour Haden and Whistler depend for their effect upon large spaces of paper being left white, and the judgment with which this is done shows mastery quite as much as the lines actually drawn. On the other hand, a pen-and-ink drawing which should attempt to give all the facts that a photograph does would certainly fail, and would only be a painful misapplication of labour.

I cannot conclude these general remarks better

than by again quoting from our great art teacher, who after telling the student not to be impatient with his pen and ink, "for all great painters, however delicate their perception of colour, are

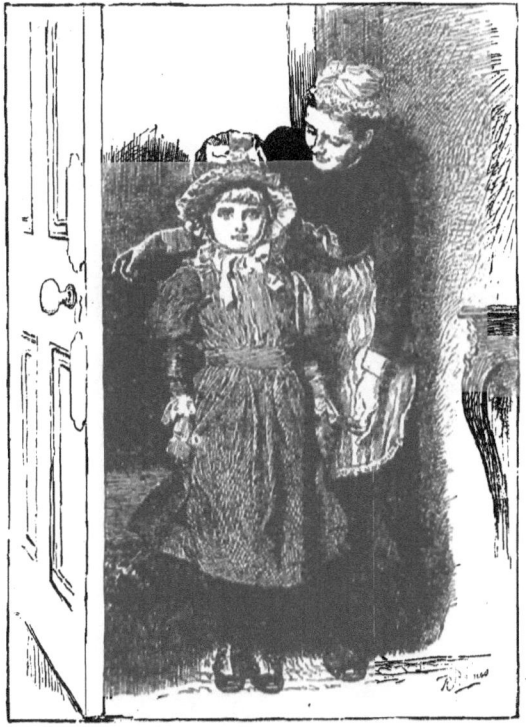

HER FIRST VISIT.—*R. Barnes.*

fond of the peculiar effect of light which may be got in a pen-and-ink sketch and in a woodcut, by the gleaming of the white paper between the black lines," adds the following emphatic piece of advice :

" Do not, therefore, think that your drawing must be weak because you have a finely pointed pen in your hand. Till you can draw with that, you can draw with nothing ; when you can draw with that you can draw with a log of wood charred at the end."

PRACTICAL INSTRUCTIONS.

DRAWING with pen and ink is so frequently called etching, and its appearance on paper is so often mistaken for a print from a copperplate, that some comparison of the technique of the two processes will not be out of place.

In etching proper the lines owe their different degrees of strength to two causes; firstly, the width of the lines produced by the use of needles of different sizes, and secondly, the depth to which they have been bitten into the copper. This latter cause regulates the quantity of ink in each line, so that if a passage in a plate is very slightly bitten, the lines printed from it will be very pale indeed. In pen-and-ink drawing we also employ the varying width of the line as a means of producing effect; and to correspond to the second cause we can dilute our ink with water, so as to make it as pale as we will. For rapidity of manipulation and perfect freedom of action the needle is unsurpassed, as it glides over the metal in all directions without the slightest trouble; but the line is uniform in character, there being no elasticity in the point of the needle such as is possessed by that of the pen. Though incapable of being handled with such celerity as the needle, yet the pen has the great charm of accentuating a line in parts, resulting from the power of separating its nibs, and thus widening the lines where required.

In outline drawing the common practice of thickening the line on the shaded side is not to be advised, as it is not based upon any sound reason, but is rather a device for smartening up the effect. Whether the extra thickness of line is added beyond or within the true contour of the object, it is

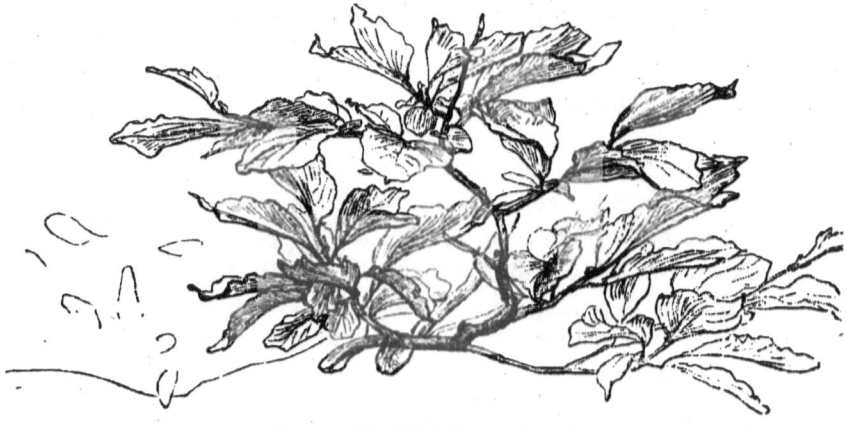

STUDY.—*Sir F. Leighton, P.R.A.*

apt to suggest a falsification of the form ; and as the extreme edge of the shaded side of most objects is seldom their darkest part, the practice is so far incorrect. Indefensible as this practice is, it is nevertheless adopted in many series of school examples, otherwise excellent in every respect ; such, for instance, as the elementary copies so much used in France, known as the Jean Cousin, L'ecolier Parisien and Raphael. This mode of

adding effeçt to a poor-looking drawing seems to
be a survival from the time when it was a great
part of the drawing-master's work to touch up his
pupils' productions in order to please their parents.
On the other hand, it is wearisome to see very
great care bestowed upon the attempt to make the
lines everywhere exactly of one thickness. When
this is very rigidly done, the result is a hard
wiriness that is no doubt scientifically right, but
is apt to look unfeeling. A little emphasis here
and there is sure to take place if the draughtsman
is thinking, as he should be, more of the properties
of the object he is portraying than of his own
manipulation. Should it be desired to produce a
bold outline of uniform width, use might be made
of a 'stylographic pen,' such as Goodall's well-
known 'Rapid Writer.'*

Mr. Ruskin, in his 'Elements of Drawing,' sets
the pupil down for a considerable time to the
simple task of laying a flat tint by means of pen
and ink. He advises the student to draw a square
and try to fill it in with crossed lines so completely
and evenly, that it shall look like a square patch
of grey silk or cloth, cut out and laid on the
white paper. He is to cover it quickly, first with
straightish lines in any direction he likes, not
troubling himself to draw them very closely or
neatly. These lines are to be crossed with other
sets of lines in all directions, care being particularly taken that each set of lines be in turn allowed

* This pen, I understand, may be obtained from the publisher
of this Handbook, price 5s.

to dry thoroughly before being crossed by another set. In this exercise swiftness of execution is recommended to avoid the dot of ink liable to be left by the pen at the end of any line which is drawn slowly, even though the pen-knife should be occasionally called into requisition to remove the ends of such lines as have gone over the edge of the square. The pen-knife should not, however, be used till the last thing ; as, where the surface of the paper has been disturbed by it, fresh lines are apt to run into blots.

A few delicate washes added to an elaborate drawing in Indian ink, will often produce a good effect by blending some of the tints together ; and by softening the shaded parts will somewhat obliterate the evidence of excessive labour. Such washes must, however, be applied with caution, care being taken not to go over any part a second time while still wet. If the brush is thus used with discrimination, the result is not unlike that produced by *retroussage* in the printing of etchings (see 'Art of Etching,' p. 46), and like it is condemned by the narrow-minded as illegitimate. Parts that are too heavy may be lightened somewhat with india-rubber, and still more with gentle use of ink-eraser.

In Mr. Hamerton's 'Graphic Arts,' attention is called to the value of "the black blot" as a technical means in pen-and-ink drawing. On this point he writes as follows : "Every reader who is at all familiar with the analysis of works of art must be aware already that in most drawings a

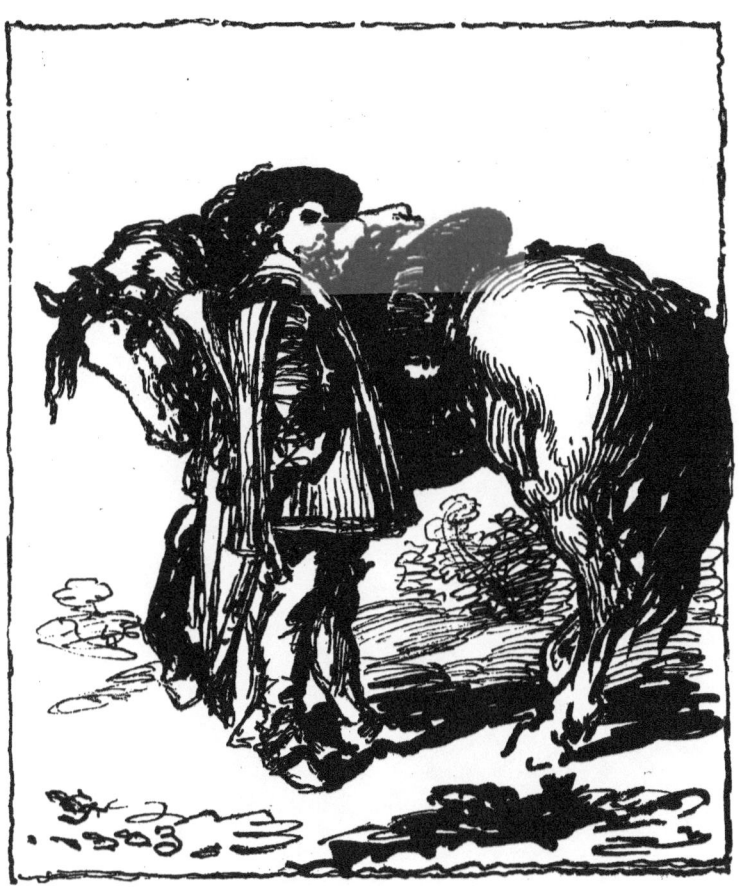

'A TRUMPETER.—*Sir John Gilbert, R.A.*

great number of light shades are lost in pure white paper. I may call his attention to the fact, which he knows quite well already, that pure white paper is absolutely *flat*, that there is no gradation in it whatever. We see, then, that in tolerating white

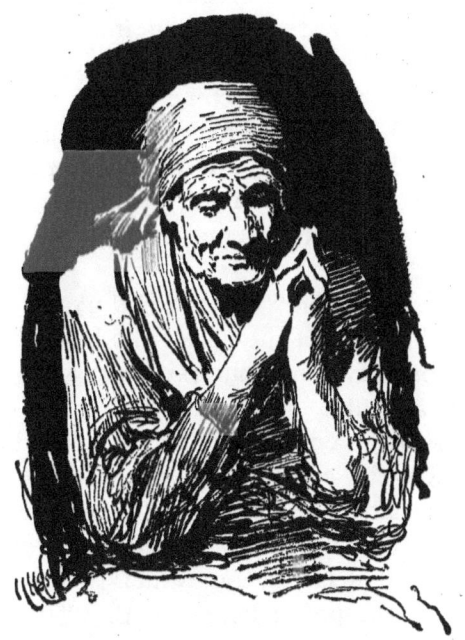

HAPPY OLD AGE.—*H. Herkomer, A.R.A.*

in a drawing, we tolerate the merging of many shades in one, which stands for them generally, as the word "aristocracy" stánds for all the higher classes; and besides this we tolerate an untruth, the abscnce of gradation, which is contrary to the habit of nature. There can be no valid reason

D

why exactly the same thing should not be done at
the other end of the scale. We have flat whites in
abundance ; why not admit flat blacks? All that
the artist means by them, is that at those places
the darks of nature went down below a certain
level. The holes and corners of picturesque build-
ings are darker than Indian ink with the light
upon it, and so are the shady side of all dark
draperies ; other darks come nearly up to Indian
ink, and others (greys and browns in nature) are
just equivalent to it. The flat black represents all
these together, quite as fairly and legitimately as
the flat white represents luminous greys and
greens."

Mr. Herkomer's " Happy Old Age," is a very
effective instance of the use of the black blot. Our
illustrations by Sir John Gilbert and Frederick
Walker are also successful examples of similar
boldness in the employment of absolute black.

Mr. Ruskin strongly advocates the invariable
use of a perfectly black ink, recommending, for
instance, ordinary writing ink that has been allowed
to stand till it has become thick (but not so much
as to clog the pen) ; believing that " if you cannot
gradate well with pure black lines, you will never
gradate well with pale ones." I confess that I see
no reasonable objection to the use of pale lines for
the purpose of obtaining gradation ; and the example
selected by Mr. Ruskin, in illustration of his
method, is somewhat unfortunate as an argument.
He tells the pupil to look at any common woodcuts
in the cheap publications of the day, and observe

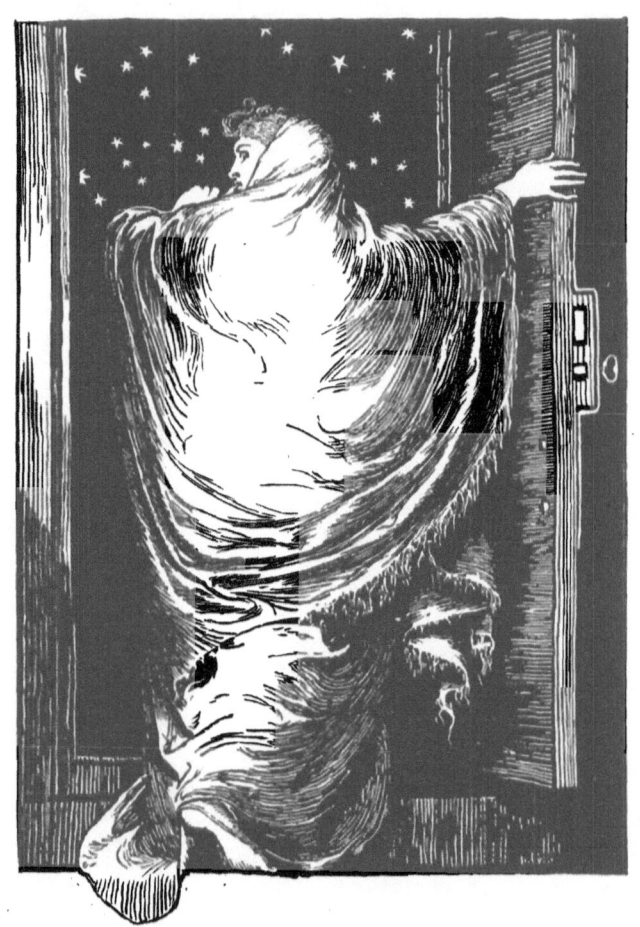

The Woman in White.—*F. Walker, R.A.*

how gradation is given to the sky by leaving the lines farther and farther apart. The fact is, that such gradation is always assisted in the printing by what is called "over-laying" the block, a system by which the pressure is regulated in such a manner as to print some parts of the block with very much more ink than others. By this means the lines in the sky are often of a decidedly pale grey, compared to the rich blacks of the dark parts of the subject. An impression of a wood-cut in which all the lines are of equal blackness is called " a rough pull," and is flat and ineffective, the sky and other delicate parts suffering most evidently from the absence of such tender gradation as can be best given by relative paleness in the ink.

A very smooth hand-made paper is perhaps the best surface for pen-and-ink drawing. The granulated surface of rough paper is apt to give the lines a broken appearance, and to hinder the free movement of the pen. There is some *old* Whatman paper existing which is excellent for the purpose ; it is rather thin, and has a beautiful surface which, however, stops short of the absolute smoothness of hot-pressed paper.

Bristol boards are perhaps the most generally useful, while London boards are to be preferred for any work not especially minute in detail. These cardboards have the advantage that the drawings made on them do not need to be mounted afterwards, and so they avoid all risk of damage while being damped and stretched.

The enamelled paper known as " clay-faced" has

come into use of late years, especially for drawings to be afterwards reproduced by photo-mechanical processes. It is said to be a coating of china clay with which the surface of the paper is prepared ; and their speciality is that black lines can be easily erased with a penknife, while white lines or dots can be added with a needle in any parts that happen to be too dark.

Messrs. Perry and Co. manufacture some pens expressly for drawing, which they have numbered thus : 600 Crow-quill pen, 601 Etching pen, and 602 Tracing pen, all these being admirably suited for fine work.

It may interest some of our readers to know that last year, and again this year, Messrs. Perry awarded prizes in a competition of drawings by amateurs, executed with their No. 600 Crow-quill pen.

Messrs. Gillott's lithographic crow-quills are much used, and this firm makes a pen specially for drawing, No. 303, and another good pen, which they call extra-fine.

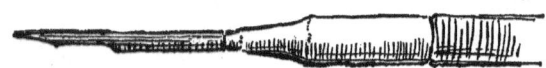

The penholder sketched on this page is made by Messrs. Woodward, who call it the IXL. ; it is convenient to the fingers, as being a holder of the usual size, while the pen is a small crow-quill. One advantage of such a pen as Gillott's extra-

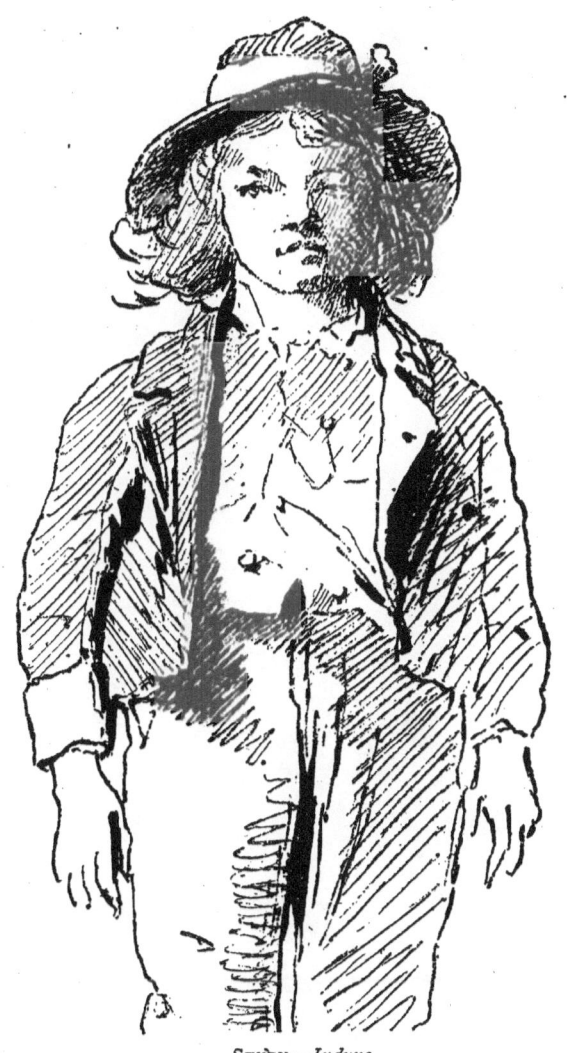

STUDY.—*Induno.*

fine over the crow-quill is that it does not require
replenishing with ink so often. It is a good plan
to use different pens for different parts of a
drawing, just as an etcher uses different needles
on different parts of his plate. All varieties of
writing pens can thus be utilized, even occasionally
the broad-nibbed J.

The preparation known by us as Indian-ink is
really of Chinese manufacture. The true China
ink will break to almost a polished surface, and is
moderately scented with musk. The counterfeits
generally overdo this ; and some neglect it altogether. The true ink is blackest when brought
to a deep shade, but in the fainter shades it inclines
to brown. The counterfeits have more substance
towards the deep shades than the genuine. The
true preserves a greater degree of transparency
than the others. Indian ink has one quality which
is sometimes found to be a disadvantage. It is
extremely difficult to remove when once applied to
the paper, being very little affected by the use of
a wet brush, sponge, or blotting paper. In this
respect, it is the antithesis of charcoal grey, which
is a beautiful pearly grey colour for monochrome,
but attaches itself to the paper so slightly that a
second wash, if not very dexterously applied, is
pretty sure to disturb the first.

The following particulars about Indian ink, ivory
black, and lamp black, are extracted from ' Field's
Chromatography for Artists.'*

" Indian ink is brought to this country in oblong

* Published by Messrs. Winsor & Newton, price 5*s.*

cakes of a musky scent, ready prepared for use with water. It varies considerably in body and colour.

"Ivory black is obtained by charring ivory in closed retorts. When well made it is the richest and most transparent of all the blacks, and is perfectly durable. If, however, insufficiently burnt, it is brown, and if too much burnt, becomes opaque and loses intensity. Ivory black is a full silky black, and is serviceable where the sooty density of lamp black would be out of place. It has a tendency to brown in its pale washes."

Lamp black is a smoke black, and is said by Mr. Field to be obtained by burning resins or resinous woods, and is defined as a pure vegetable charcoal of fine texture. I believe, however, that at the present time, lamp black is usually manufactured by the burning of some of the many varieties of petroleum, chemically called hydrocarbons. Perhaps for the finest qualities, resinous woods may be still employed. It is not quite so intense and transparent as ivory black, but less brown in its pale washes.

Liquid brown ink is gradually becoming popular, particularly for the purpose of perspective elevations of architects. Washes of this ink can be used along with the ordinary work of the pen. Capital examples of this employment of brown ink have been exhibited lately at the Royal Academy by Mr. Ernest George. When compared with the other elevations outlined and tinted either with Indian ink or sepia, those in brown ink certainly

look the most effective. The warm tone of the
brown ink, as used in this manner, is decidedly
agreeable. These drawings of Mr. George reproduce very fairly by photo-lithography, though
with some slight exaggeration of the lighter washes.

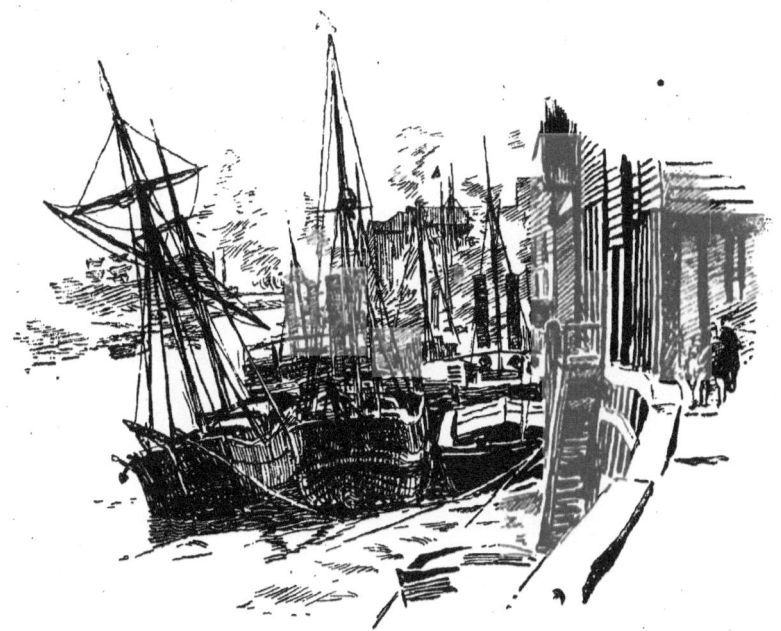

HULL.—*W. L. Wyllie.*

The superiority of brown over black for the
purposes of decorative effect has recently been
very fully recognised in the selection of the ink
used in printing such etchings as those of Mr.
Macbeth after Mason, Pinwell, and Walker.

Besides liquid Indian ink and brown ink ready

for use, Messrs. Winsor & Newton keep cakes or sticks of the best Nankin Indian ink in great variety. The following is a list of their selection, varying in price from fourteen shillings down to sixpence per stick : Extra large Double Dragon, Hexagon, Super-super, Mandarin, Pearl, Stork gilt, Square gilt, Lion's head, besides smaller sizes of several of these brands. We may mention that the Super-super and Lion's head brands are in practice found to be the most generally useful.

REPRODUCTIVE PROCESSES.

THE immense strides made lately in the processes of mechanical reproduction tend to show that the art of pen-and-ink drawing is becoming every day more worth attention on its own account. As a definite method of artistic expression, it seems not unlikely that, in the future, as the processes alluded to approach perfection, the intermediate part played by the wood-engraver will be superseded by them ; and that all our illustrated newspapers and periodicals will only require suitable designs from artists for photographic reproduction.

The most direct way, however, in which pen-and-ink drawings may be made for the purpose of reproduction, is on lithographic stone, zinc, or by the use of what is called "transfer-paper" in connection with lithography or zincography. This transfer-paper is yellow-coloured in appearance, being prepared for its purpose by being coated with a mixture of gum arabic, gamboge, &c. The preparation admits of the use of the ordinary black-lead pencil for sketching in the design, or a tracing may be made on it by means of red chalk tracing-paper that has been made in the most simple manner without any greasy admixture. The drawing is made with lithographic transfer ink, when it must be borne in mind that·the process takes no notice of differing degrees of black in the line, but only in the width of the line. The drawing is transferred by the paper being damped at the back, and placed face downwards on the lithographic stone or zinc plate, and then passed through a press of considerable power. The paper can now be peeled off, and the drawing is left adhering to the stone or plate, from which it can be printed in the usual manner.

There is, besides the ordinary yellow transfer-paper, another kind, known as " French transparent," which serves the purpose of a tracing as well as a transfer paper. The use of the sable brush (as figured on p. 50) is preferable to that of the pen, which is liable to abrade the preparation on the surface of these papers.

Great care must be observed in using these transfer papers, not to touch the surface with the hands, as the slightest soil of grease, although it may not be apparent, will ink up black when transferred.

Messrs. Cattell, the well-known zincographers, recommend the ink called " Vanhymbeck's Autographic Transfer Ink," and they give the following simple directions for mixing the ink : " Warm a small saucer over the gas or a candle, then rub the ink round it until a sufficient quantity has adhered to the saucer, which it will do, in the form of a thick paste ; then add a few drops of distilled, rain, or boiled water, mixing well with the finger until liquid enough to flow freely from the brush or pen ; not too thick, or it will smash in transferring, nor too thin, or the lines will not come out properly."

In pen-and-ink drawing on stone, or on paper

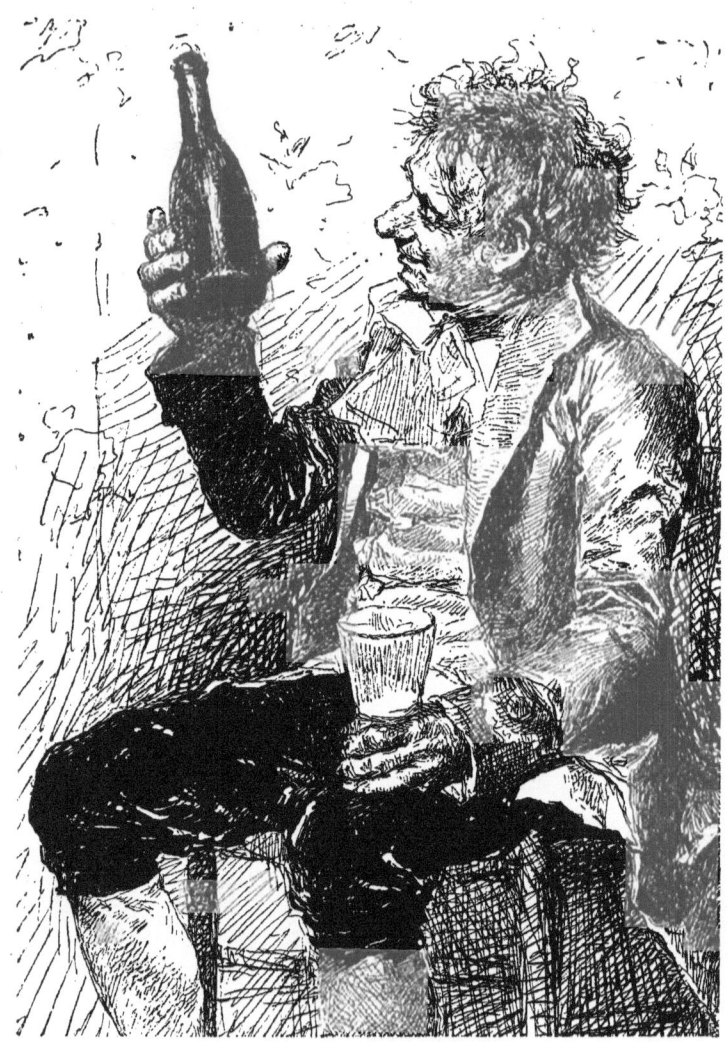

A Vintage Wine.—*Simonetti.*

for lithographic transfer, it must be recollected that the strength of the line depends entirely upon its thickness, as the ink when printed is everywhere uniform in blackness ; so that such work corresponds to an etching produced with only one immersion in the acid, and to a pen-and-ink drawing on paper where the pen is always kept fully charged with ink of the same intensity. The same thing also holds good with reference to the pen-and-ink drawings so frequently made for one or other of the photo-type processes now so much employed—in Mr. Blackburn's 'Academy Notes,' for instance.

The best ink with which to draw for these processes, or more correctly, better than any ink, is the preparation known as " Stephens' Ebony Stain." It has more body than any simple ink ; while, at the same time, it is not thickened to such a degree as to prevent the pen or brush from making the very finest lines. I have tried many good writing inks, such as " Carter's Raven Black," but have found nothing in strength to compare with the Ebony Stain. Some draughtsmen mix a little gamboge with Indian ink, so as to render the black more suitable for photography. An ink inclining to blue should be particularly avoided, as not likely to photograph well.

The paper for " process " drawing should be very smooth, such as Bristol board. The best thing, however, is a particular kind of prepared cardboard known as " clay-faced," which is sold at the establishments that supply materials for these processes.

E

Messrs. Willis & Co., of Long Acre, keep this
prepared cardboard in stock.

For such work in pure line as is required to be
very exact for purposes of publication, it is not
unusual to employ a finely-pointed sable brush
instead of a pen, the result produced being so
similar that few would imagine they were not
looking at a pen-and-ink drawing.   The sable
brushes known as 'tracers,' 'liners,' or 'riggers,' are

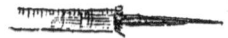

specially adapted to this kind of work, all of them
being very long in proportion to their thickness.
Any small sable brush may be trimmed with a
sharp penknife to the required proportion as shown
in the accompanying illustration.   Their shape
facilitates the task of shading by means of parallel
lines of regular width.   It is by no means easy at
first to use the brush in this way as a substitute
for the pen, and it is only suitable for work that is
to be done very deliberately.   Were one to attempt
sudden alterations in the direction of the lines, such
as are easy enough with the pen, the result with
the brush would most probably be a succession of
blots.   With practice, however, considerable rapidity
may be acquired ; and those who have once become
accustomed to the use of the brush as a substitute
for the pen, are never known to recur to the use of
the latter.

In this method of working, such pigments as
Indian ink, lamp black, ivory black, are used

instead of fluid ink, the only exception being in favour of Stephens' Ebony Stain, which is equally suited to the pen or the brush. From experiments that I made in order to test the relative intensity of different inks and pigments, I came to the conclusion that lamp black as prepared for water colour and used with the brush produced the most perfect black of all. The apparent reason for this is, not that the pigment is really deeper in shade than the others ; but that owing to a complete absence of shine on its surface it takes no reflection from surrounding objects, and so remains a perfectly dead black at whatever angle it may be held to the light. In practice, Stephens' Ebony Stain, though yielding a somewhat shining surface, is found to photograph quite satisfactorily. The presence of red in this preparation, probably logwood, which may be readily seen by adding a few drops to a tumbler of water, no doubt materially improves its quality as a colour intended to photograph as dark as possible.

In making designs to be reproduced by photomechanical processes, it is usual to draw them considerably larger than they are to be eventually printed. This proceeding, by rendering all the lines finer and closer, adds a general appearance of delicacy and finish to the whole. Experience, however, shows that this added finish of execution does not necessarily mean finish of effect, for where great difference of scale exists between the original and the reproduction, the balance of tone is altered and frequently upset. A warning on this subject

E 2

appeared in 'Harper's Magazine,' from the pen of
Mr. Thomas Cole, one of the ablest living wood
engravers. He writes, " The secret of so many
recent failures of engravers to do justice to the
artist lies in the fact that artists make their
drawings too large, and when these are reduced
by photography and put on the block very small
the engraver is put to a great task in striving to
reproduce the original effect ; and he fails in the endeavour because through the reduction in size the
effect has been lost !" The greys, which will probably
compose the chief part of the design, remain sub-
stantially the same, while the whites and blacks dimi-
nish in importance, so that the usual result when a
drawing has been made on a large scale, is, that the
reduction is pronounced weak or grey throughout.

In my own practice, I generally like to make my
drawings for " photographic reduction " to a scale
of about twice the linear measurement required ;
in other words, four times the area. If, for
instance, the size of the illustrations is to be six
inches in height, I should prefer to make my
drawings twelve inches ; but I should be careful in
these cases to keep the work very open, and the
white and black spaces larger than would look well
on the scale I was using. To work in this way
requires some effort and constant self control, so as
not to put in too much work ; the result is that
most artists find it on the whole less troublesome
to work on a scale nearer to that of the intended
reduction. Mr. Staniland and others, who have
been very successful in this class of work, find that

if the linear measurement is one-third larger than the reduction, the latter is found to be sensibly improved in the direction of delicacy without much

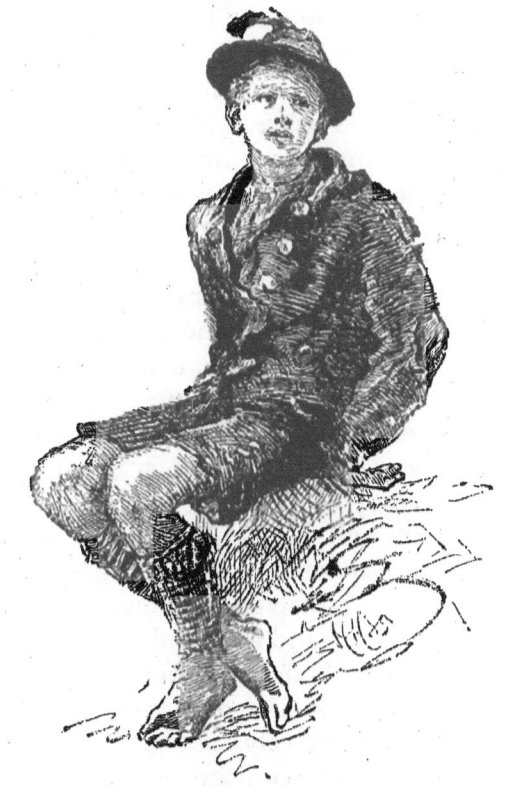

BOY RESTING.—*H. Herkomer, A.R.A.*

alteration of general effect. Supposing, as before, that the illustrations are to be six inches in height, the artists alluded to would probably draw them about eight inches. The reduction in this case

would be half the area, though a casual observer
would not fancy it to be nearly so considerable.   I
may mention that the original of Mr. East's
impressive drawing of the 'Dark Island,' (p. 13),
measured about 13 inches by 9, and my own pen-
and-ink drawing of 'Grig-weels,' (p. 62), nearly
filled a page of note paper.   Mr. Blackburn has on
the whole found that those drawings which do not
exceed the size of an ordinary sheet of note paper
come out best on the small scale to which they are
reduced in 'Academy Notes.'

    The question as to how many parallel lines in a
given space will present to the naked eye the appearance of a flat tint or wash, becomes of interest
when considering this part of our subject.   From
the different examples that I have examined with
this view, I have found that from 108 to 120 in the
inch are generally required to produce the effect.
These numbers will no doubt vary in particular
cases, owing to the relative width of the black and
white spaces, and to the varying powers of the eyes
of different persons ; and they will vary in *all* cases
with the distance of the lines from the eye.   The
most curious thing in the matter of these experiments is the comparatively sudden change in effect
that occurs when the requisite number of lines is
reached.   Thus, perhaps, when comparing the
effect of 96 lines to the inch with that of 108, it will
appear as if the proportionate difference must be
very great indeed, and would probably be guessed
at a fourth less, instead of being, as it is, only one
ninth.   When laying with the pen or brush an even

shade consisting of parallel lines, it will be found that about eighty lines to the inch are as many as can be laid without the aid of the magnifying glass, or devoting over much time to mere minuteness. At this rate an inch and a half would contain 120 lines, and as that number of lines when reduced to an inch would, as stated above, cause the effect of the separate lines to merge into that of a flat tint or wash, we find that the degree of reduction desirable on this ground is one-fourth, which is that already mentioned as having been frequently adopted by artists on general grounds.

It may seem paradoxical to allege that extremely fine work looks still finer under a glass of high magnifying power ; but the fact seems to be that in some respects the hand of the practised draughtsman outstrips his eye. Under the magnifying glass it may be noticed that in the case of very closely laid parallel lines, the white spaces between the lines are generally twice as wide as the lines themselves ; and so that the lines are relatively thinner or finer than they appear to the naked eye.

A curious fact has come under my observation while trying upon my friends the effect of tints composed of parallel lines ; my object being to see how many lines in a given space were required to suggest the appearance of a wash of grey colour. I was, of course, prepared to find considerable difference in the clearness of vision of different individuals, all of whom supposed themselves to have exceptionally good sight. The strange point that came under my notice is that to many persons

the same tint of parallel lines produced quite a
different effect when the paper was held so as to
present the lines horizontally, from what it did
when the lines were perpendicular; the commonest
case being that what appeared a flat wash when
the lines were horizontal, would resolve itself into
distinct lines when turned, so that the lines were
perpendicular. In other words one might put it
that perpendicular lines are more easily seen than
horizontal ones. In all eyes the central parts of
the retina are more sensitive than the peripheral
parts ; and the above-described difference of effect
may be due to the fact that, in most eyes, this
decrease of sensibility takes place more rapidly in
a vertical than in a horizontal direction.

When drawing for " process," I would give the
reader a caution not to go over the light parts of
the drawing with either pen-knife or ink-eraser for
the purpose of adding delicacy of effect. The
interference with the photographic result is much
greater than would naturally be anticipated ; the
lines after this treatment, tending to become broken,
(or rotten as it is called) to an extraordinary
degree. This course is the more to be avoided,
as after the process block is completed, the delicate parts, if too dark, can easily be rendered
greyer by being crossed with finely engraved lines ;
but no breaks in a line can be afterwards supplied.

For photo-type reproduction a combination of
pen-and-ink drawing with a tint composed of ruled
lines is frequently adopted. This is an easy method
of obtaining tone, and getting rid of the unfinished

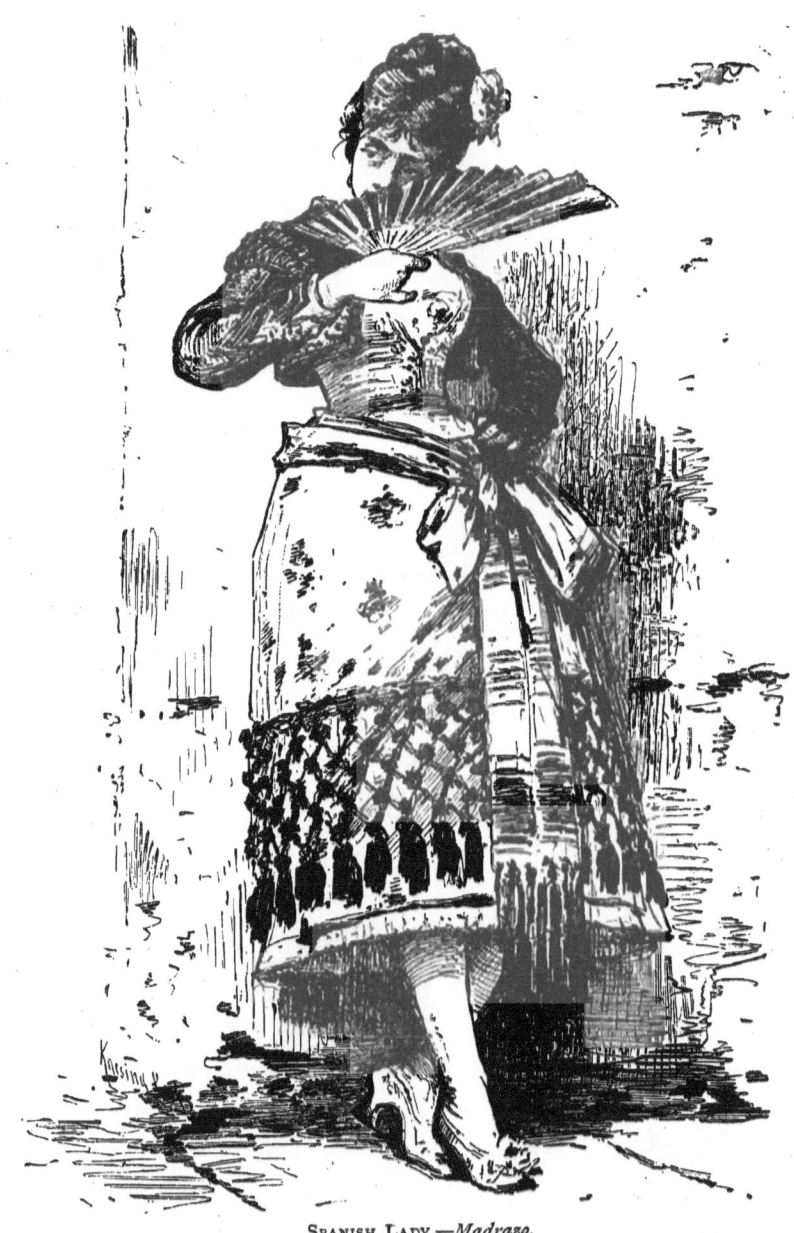

SPANISH LADY.—*Madrazo.*

appearance that a slight pen-and-ink sketch is apt
to present. As the ruled tint can be scraped away
in parts, the high lights can be expressed with
great facility. Several designs executed in this manner have appeared in Mr. Blackburn's 'Academy
Notes ;' for instance, 'The Secret,' by E. Blair
Leighton, in the volume for 1885. Reference to this
example will, I think, show that the result is not quite
satisfactory, owing to the various tones not blending
altogether harmoniously; the very great difference
in the technical methods by which the varieties of
tone are produced is no doubt the reason. It is
possible that with great care harmony of execution
might be attained ; but it would take an amount of
slow deliberate work that would be better bestowed
by adopting some other mode. The fact is, that
patches of white on a tint are apt to have an
artificial effect, unless the high lights are led up to
very gradually. Instances of this failure in harmony of effect are to be noticed in the many lithographs that used to be printed on a buff tint, with
the high lights scraped out to imitate the effect of
white chalk. These pretty lithographs, which were
so much admired in the last generation, are very
little esteemed at present ; and we will hope that it
is owing to an improved taste intolerant of their
prevalent fault of sacrificing truth to superficial
qualities.

It might seem almost unnecessary, when writing
on the subject of the reduction of drawings by
photography, to dwell on the fact of the obvious
increase of the number of lines in a given space ;

but it seems in practice extremely difficult at first
to make the necessary allowance for the difference
in this particular that must take place. I have
heard more than one accomplished artist complain
bitterly of the loss of style incurred by the mere
fact of having employed more lines to produce a
certain effect than were really needed. When the
reduction is to be considerable, it must be borne in
mind that the treatment on the large scale, to be
really right for the purpose, should not look perfectly right when the intention is not understood.
It should be decidedly coarse in execution in parts ;
and, as I have elsewhere remarked, the principal
lights and darks should be exaggerated in size.
Even to those draughtsmen who are perfectly
aware of the changes in effect that will result from
the contemplated reduction in size, the temptation
sometimes arises to make the drawings on the
large scale as attractive and as finished-looking as
possible, so that they may pass muster at a glance
with editors or publishers. Few people, except
professional artists, are found to complain of any
work of art being over-laboured ; indeed, it is by
no means a rare thing to hear a drawing praised
enthusiastically for the absurd reason that "there
is so much work in it ! "

A student who has not the opportunity of seeing
the originals of successful reductions by " process "
might perhaps learn something by inverting the
method. By choosing a good published example,
and having some photographic enlargements made
from it, he would see just how much more open

the lines would then appear, according to the scale
used ; and so he could regulate his own proceed-
ings with tolerable certainty.

While considering this aspect of our subject, I
would point out that many engravings from drawings which are commonly spoken of as pen-and-
ink sketches are not really so. For example, it is
not unusual to hear John Leech's sketches in
'Punch,' spoken of in this way ; and certainly some
of his later ones are not unlike what might have been
done with a quill-pen. The fact is that they were
drawn on the wood with grey lead-pencil, and were
not at all powerful-looking in that state, depending
as they did for their after-effect more upon the
actual width of the lines than their tone on the wood.

A curious and ingenious invention has recently
come to us from Australia, known as "Crocker's Hot
Pen." A hollow pen-holder, filled with wax, is connected with the gas supply by a piece of India-
rubber tubing, so that a tiny jet of gas is kept
burning just above the pen. This melts the wax
and enables it to pass down the nibs of the pen in
a fluid state. The drawing is made upon glass or
other smooth cold surface, upon which the wax
solidifies the instant it leaves the pen. The drawing is thus composed of raised lines of wax instead
of ink. An electro deposit of copper is made upon
this which forms a plate in reverse ; that is, the
lines in the electro are sunken to the degree that
they were raised in the original, and the depth is
found to be quite as great as that produced by
etching with acid. This invention is also available

for the production of surface-printing blocks by the simple means of immersing the drawing on glass in a bath of fluoric acid, when all the parts not drawn upon will be lowered by its corrosive action.

I have not myself tried this process, but judging from the specimens I have seen of it, I conclude that it would be difficult to do fine work slowly by it ; the natural tendency being for all deliberately laid lines to come thick, while quickly scribbled ones seem to come thin in proportion to the rapidity with which they are done. The method is, however, very simple, and saves all the trouble connected with the use of acid ; and I do not see why a plate thus executed should not receive the addition of lightly etched work where desirable, or delicate lines done with the dry-point.

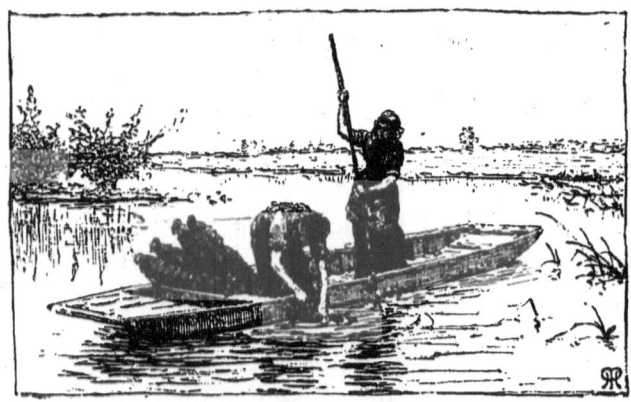

GRIG-WEELS.—*H. R. Robertson.*